Original title:
Snowbound in Warmth

Copyright © 2024 Creative Arts Management OÜ
All rights reserved.

Author: Jaxon Kingsley
ISBN HARDBACK: 978-9916-94-432-5
ISBN PAPERBACK: 978-9916-94-433-2

Against the Frost

The world is wrapped in icy breath,
Trees stand still, a shivering death.
Snowflakes dance on the frozen ground,
A quiet chill, with silence found.

We gather close, our spirits bright,
In hearth's embrace, we chase the night.
Against the frost, our warmth ignites,
In shadows cast, we share our lights.

Silent Warmth

In winter's grip, with whispers low,
A flame ignites, a gentle glow.
We cuddle close, our hearts entwined,
In hidden corners, love designed.

Through frosty panes, the stars do gleam,
In twilight hours, we softly dream.
With every breath, a silent song,
In warmth we find where we belong.

The Comfort of Coziness

Wrapped in blankets, soft and warm,
Outside, the storm may do its harm.
A steaming cup, the fire's glow,
In cozy nooks, our laughter flows.

With each shared story, time stands still,
Embracing peace, with hearts to fill.
Beneath the weight of winter's veil,
In comfortable bonds, we prevail.

Embracing the Icy Veil

The world is draped in ice's lace,
A crystal scene, a frozen place.
We wander onward, hand in hand,
Embracing all, the winter's brand.

With every step, the snowflakes sigh,
A beauty found beneath the sky.
In chilly air, our laughter rings,
In icy realms, our spirit swings.

Winter's Embrace

Snowflakes dance in silent flight,
Blanketing earth in purest white.
Trees stand tall, cloaked in frost,
Nature's beauty, never lost.

The air is crisp with winter's breath,
Whispers echo of life and death.
Stars twinkle in the night sky bright,
Guiding souls through the wintry night.

Cozy Hearth Whispers

The crackling fire softly glows,
Casting shadows, where the warmth flows.
Blankets wrapped, we sit so near,
In the hearth's light, all is clear.

Stories shared and laughter bright,
Moments cherished in the night.
With each sip of cocoa warm,
Love and joy become the norm.

Frosted Tales by Flickering Light

Stories woven in the dark,
Frosty windows, a glowing spark.
Children's laughter fills the room,
Chasing away the winter's gloom.

By the fire, tales come alive,
Of brave hearts and dreams that thrive.
Every crackle, each soft sigh,
As time slips past, we wonder why.

Embracing the Chill

The world is wrapped in icy lace,
Every breath a visible trace.
Hats pulled tight and gloves adorned,
In winter's chill, our spirits warmed.

We walk through drifts, a frosty maze,
Finding joy in winter's gaze.
Embracing cold with hearts aglow,
Together we brave the frost and snow.

Where Hearts Stay Cozy

In the glow of the fire's light,
Where whispers dance through the night,
Hearts entwined like vines of spring,
Love's warm song, forever we sing.

Outside the world may chill and freeze,
Yet here we find our gentle ease,
With every laugh and shared embrace,
In cozy corners, we find our place.

Flickers of Change

Leaves whisper secrets in the breeze,
Colors shift with such subtle ease,
Life unfolds, a story anew,
With every dawn, dreams break through.

Paths once hidden now brightly show,
Seeds of tomorrow start to sow,
In moments brief, we find our way,
Flickers of hope greet each new day.

Warm Nights in the Frost

Under stars that shimmer and gleam,
The world is quiet, lost in a dream,
Wrapped in blankets, hearts feel light,
Warm nights glow in the frosty night.

Laughter echoes in the chilly air,
A bond so strong, nothing can compare,
With every story shared and told,
The warmth of love, more precious than gold.

Winter's Embrace

Snowflakes fall like softest lace,
Each one unique in its own place,
Nature's blanket, pure and white,
Winter wraps us, soft and tight.

In the silence, peace unfolds,
A winter tale of love retold,
Together we stand against the cold,
In winter's embrace, our hearts are bold.

Warmth in the Stillness

In quiet corners, shadows dance,
A gentle breeze, a fleeting chance.
The whispered hush of evening light,
Embraces all, dispels the night.

With every breath, a warmth unfolds,
In cozy nooks, the heart consoles.
A cup of joy, steam rising high,
In stillness here, our spirits fly.

The world outside may chill and sigh,
Yet here within, our souls comply.
A tapestry of dreams and whispers,
In the stillness, joy persists.

We hold each moment, close and near,
In cozy spaces, free from fear.
Together, finding peace anew,
In warmth's embrace, just me and you.

Frosted Paths to Warmth

Through fields where frost lays silver white,
We walk together, hearts alight.
Each step we take, the crunching sound,
Leads us to warmth, true love unbound.

The frosted paths tell tales of yore,
Of winter's chill and heart's encore.
Together, we embrace the cold,
With hands held tight, our warmth unfolds.

In every glimmer, hope shines clear,
With frosty breath, we draw near.
Each moment shared, a treasured find,
On paths of frost, our hearts entwined.

So let the winter winds entwine,
As we stroll under starlit shine.
For in the cold, our fire ignites,
With every step, our spirits light.

Sanctuary in Softness

In tender folds of downy grace,
We find a refuge, a sacred space.
The whispers soft, like lullabies,
In gentle arms, our worries fly.

The world outside, a distant hue,
But here we breathe, just me and you.
With cushions wrapped around our dreams,
In this sanctuary, peace redeems.

The clock may tick, the hours drift,
Yet in this warmth, we find our lift.
A soft embrace, a refuge true,
In every moment, I see you.

Together sheltered, time stands still,
In quiet corners, we can chill.
This sanctuary, our hearts will claim,
In softness found, we stoke the flame.

Where Frost Meets Fire

In the twilight where shadows blend,
Frost and fire, a dance unbends.
The chilly breath of winter's night,
Meets the warmth of a flickering light.

Each breath of frost, a crisp caress,
While flames erupt, a bold finesse.
This meeting place of chill and glow,
Creates a magic only we know.

The fire crackles, stories shared,
In each warm flicker, love declared.
As frost nips softly at our feet,
The flames embrace, where hearts do meet.

So let us linger, just you and I,
As frosted whispers brush the sky.
In this sweet fusion, we both aspire,
To find our bliss where frost meets fire.

Hearthstone Dreams

In the glow of amber light,
Warmth whispers through the night.
Crackling fire, shadows dance,
In its glow, lost in a trance.

Memories like embers glow,
Stories shared, a gentle flow.
Family gathered, hearts entwined,
In this place, love defined.

Outside, the chill winds wail,
Inside, the warmth will prevail.
Hearthstone dreams cradle the soul,
In this refuge, we feel whole.

The Softness of Frost

Morning whispers, blankets white,
Frosty whispers, soft and light.
Each breath visible, a sweet ballet,
Nature's canvas, a delicate display.

Trees adorned in sparkling lace,
Time slows down in frosty grace.
Footsteps crunch on icy ground,
In silence, winter's magic found.

Frosted petals, gentle glow,
Kisses from the moonlit snow.
Magic lingers, sparkles bloom,
In the air, winter's perfume.

Radiance of a Winter's Hearth

In the heart of winter's chill,
The hearth's blaze ignites, a thrill.
Flickering flames that leap and sway,
Chasing shadows, keeping gloom at bay.

A gentle family rendezvous,
With stories shared and laughter too.
This sacred space, a sacred bond,
In the warmth of love, we're fond.

Outside, the world is cold and bare,
Inside, joy and warmth we share.
Radiance glows in every heart,
A winter's dream, where we won't part.

Melted Hearts

Warmed by sun, the ice will break,
Winter's grip begins to shake.
With each ray, the world transforms,
As melted hearts embrace the warm.

Flowing rivers, songs of spring,
Nature wakes, its joy takes wing.
Laughter dances in the air,
Love's fresh bloom, beyond compare.

Cloaked in colors bright and bold,
Stories of the season told.
Gentle whispers, soft and clear,
Melted hearts draw friends near.

Winterscape of Light

Snowflakes dance in twilight's glow,
Whispers soft, where cold winds blow.
Stars above in silent flight,
Crafting dreams in winter's night.

Moonlight casts its silver thread,
Covering paths where shadows tread.
Branches glisten, draped in white,
A still world, aglow with light.

Stillness Wrapped in Warmth

The fire crackles, soft and bright,
Encasing us in cozy light.
Blankets piled, hearts entwined,
Finding peace, our solace confined.

Outside, frost paints the window clear,
While laughter lingers, we hold dear.
Time stands still, with love so vast,
In this moment, we are steadfast.

Unearthed Warmth

From depths of winter's frozen spell,
Awakens warmth, a secret swell.
Beneath the ice, life stirs and sighs,
A promise blooms in sunny skies.

As days grow bright, the earth will cheer,
Revealing colors, crystal clear.
Hope emerges, soft and bold,
Unearthed warmth, a tale retold.

The Warmth of a Whisper

In twilight's gentle hold, we find,
The secrets shared, a love so kind.
Soft echoes dance upon the air,
A promise whispered, hearts laid bare.

Through shadowed nights, your voice a balm,
A tender touch, a soothing calm.
In every word, a world anew,
Together bound, just me and you.

Beneath the stars, the night unfolds,
Each whisper spun from tales of old.
An intimacy, fine as lace,
In every breath, your warm embrace.

Let silence linger, let it thieve,
For in this hush, we truly breathe.
With whispered thoughts, our spirits soar,
In softest tones, we ask for more.

Haven of Hearth

In the corner, the fire glows bright,
Casting shadows that dance with delight.
A sanctuary, warm and near,
Cradled in love, banishing fear.

The kettle sings a song of old,
Sweet aroma of stories told.
Hearts entwined like flames that play,
In this haven, we find our way.

Flickering light and laughter blend,
Time stands still, as moments mend.
Wrapped in blankets, we find our peace,
In the hearth's embrace, our joys increase.

As twilight dims and stars arise,
We gaze upon the endless skies.
In this shelter, forever stay,
Where love ignites and lights our way.

Frosted Glass and Glowing Hearts

Through frosted panes, the world outside,
A winter's chill, where secrets hide.
Yet in our hearts, a fire gleams,
A warmth that shines, fulfilling dreams.

Snowflakes dance in moonlight's glow,
Each flake a story, fresh and slow.
In every crystal, memories spun,
A tapestry of love begun.

With hands entwined, we brave the cold,
In laughter shared, our dreams unfold.
The world may freeze, but here we stand,
In glowing hearts, forever planned.

So let the winds howl, let the night wail,
In our cocoon, we shall not fail.
For in this space, two souls shall glide,
On frosted glass, love will abide.

Tiny Flames in Winter's Grip

Winter's breath wraps the world so tight,
Yet within, we kindled a small light.
Tiny flames that flicker and dance,
In their warmth, we take a chance.

Each spark a story, softly told,
Against the chill, we stand so bold.
In shadows cast, our spirits rise,
Glimmers bright beneath vast skies.

The nights grow long, the cold winds sigh,
Yet here we sit, just you and I.
With each small flame, our hopes revive,
A testament to love alive.

For while the frost may grip the land,
Our hearts ignite, with strength we stand.
In tiny flames, a fire grows,
Through winter's bite, our passion flows.

Frosted Memories

Whispers of winter dance on the breeze,
Footprints in snow, like secrets, they tease.
Silent reflections in the moon's soft glow,
Memories flicker like frost on the window.

Branches adorned in a delicate lace,
Each flake a story, a time, a place.
The chill wraps around, yet warms the heart,
Frosted memories, where dreams never part.

Embraced by Softness

In cozy corners, where shadows reside,
Blankets enfold me, a cushy abide.
The world fades away into whispers and sighs,
Embraced by softness under gentle skies.

Cocoa steam rising, a sweet, warm embrace,
Each sip a reminder of love's gentle grace.
Time slows as I drift in this tranquil space,
Wrapped in the warmth that memories trace.

Radiant Chill

A brisk wind travels, bold and free,
Leaves twirl and dance, a wild jubilee.
In the heart of winter, brilliance stands still,
Nature's own canvas in radiant chill.

Sparkling ice coats each branch with delight,
A crystalline world gleams under the light.
Gone are the shadows, the gloom, and the gray,
Radiant chill warms the coldest of days.

Comfort Amidst the Cold

The fire crackles; shadows play on the wall,
A haven of warmth when the world starts to fall.
Outside, the blizzard sings lullabies bold,
Yet here, we find comfort amidst the cold.

With laughter and stories, we gather near,
The chill may surround us, but we feel no fear.
Together we stand, in this cozy fold,
Finding our solace, comfort amid the cold.

Chilled Radiance

The moonlight dances on the frost,
A silver glow, a beauty crossed.
Whispers of night in the cool air,
Nature's secrets everywhere.

Stars twinkle, a distant choir,
Wrapped in warmth, we do aspire.
Each breath a mist, a fleeting trace,
In winter's arms, we find our grace.

Trees adorned in crystal white,
Branches sparkling, pure delight.
A tranquil world, so hushed, so still,
As shadows lengthen, hearts do fill.

A night like this, so calm, profound,
Where peace and wonder can be found.
In chilled radiance, we stand in awe,
Of nature's beauty without flaw.

Toasty Dreams

Fires crackle in the night,
Casting warmth, a soft, warm light.
Blankets wrapped around us tight,
In toasty dreams, we take flight.

Sipping cocoa, sweet surprise,
Warmth reflecting in our eyes.
Whispers shared beneath the stars,
No worries here, no heavy scars.

Snowflakes dance on windowpanes,
While outside, winter softly reigns.
Inside, love's glow brings us near,
In every laugh, in every cheer.

As evening deepens, shadows play,
In toasty dreams, we drift away.
Together here, we find our way,
In warmth and joy, we choose to stay.

Winter's Gentle Caress

Softly falls the snow at night,
Blanketing the world in white.
Winter's breath, a whispered sigh,
A gentle touch from the sky.

Each flake glistens like a star,
Nature's beauty, near and far.
A quiet peace takes hold of me,
In winter's caress, I am free.

Frozen streams in quiet gleam,
Reflecting light, a tranquil dream.
Gentle winds through branches sway,
Winter's love, in every way.

In this stillness, hearts align,
With nature's pulse, so pure, divine.
Winter's gentle touch, we trust,
In every moment, love is just.

Frozen Sanctuary

In a world where silence reigns,
Icicles hang like crystal chains.
A frozen sanctuary unfolds,
A tale of beauty, timeless, bold.

Mountains rise, majestically high,
Touching softly the winter sky.
Peace embraces all that seems,
In this place of winter dreams.

Footsteps crunch on powdery snow,
Each sound a tune, a soft hello.
Nature resting, taking pause,
In this sanctuary, without cause.

As twilight gathers, shadows play,
The world transforms at the end of day.
In frozen beauty, we shall stay,
In nature's heart, we find our way.

Embracing the Frosted Light

In the hush of morning's gleam,
Frosted whispers softly beam,
Silent trees in silver dress,
Nature's peace a soft caress.

Footprints crunch on icy trails,
Winter's breath in gentle gales,
Every glint a story told,
In this tapestry of cold.

Sunrise paints the world in gold,
Through the chill, our dreams unfold,
Hand in hand we face the dawn,
Embracing light, never gone.

Ashes and Icy Breath

In shadows where the embers lie,
Frost defies the evening sky,
Murmurs of the fire's last glow,
Breathe in deep, let the cold flow.

Every sigh a tale of loss,
Ashes whisper 'neath the frost,
Yet beneath the frozen hue,
Life awakens, pure and new.

Winter's grasp can't steal the spark,
In the heart, it leaves a mark,
From the ashes, warmth will rise,
Through icy breath, hope never dies.

Glowing Hearts in a Crystal World

Within this realm of frost and light,
Hearts aglow in the chilly night,
Each laughter shared, like crystals bright,
We find our warmth, our shared delight.

Every snowflake, unique in flight,
Dances softly, pure and white,
Together we weave through the day,
In this crystal world we play.

With twinkling stars as our guide,
In winter's charm, we will abide,
Through the cold, our spirits soar,
Glowing hearts forevermore.

Winter's Gentle Cradle

Cradled in the arms of night,
Winter whispers, cold yet bright,
Hushed beneath a blanket thick,
Time slows down, the world a trick.

Quiet moments softly weave,
Tales of joy and hearts that grieve,
In the stillness, dreams take flight,
Holding close the starry light.

Snowflakes fall like whispered prayers,
Wrapped in warmth, we shed our cares,
In winter's gentle, tender embrace,
We find our peace, our sacred space.

Cocoas and Candlelight

In the glow of candlelight,
Warm cocoa in hand,
Whispers of sweet delight,
As shadows dance and stand.

The winter chill outside,
Keeps the world at bay,
While we sit side by side,
In our own cozy fray.

The fragrance of the steam,
Fills the air with hope,
In this sweet little dream,
Together we can cope.

With laughter and soft sighs,
Time slows down its race,
In this world where love lies,
We have found our place.

Heartbeats in the Frostbite

In the stillness of the night,
Frost bites at the skin,
Yet our hearts beat bright,
As warmth lies deep within.

The stars above us gleam,
Captured in the ice,
While we weave a dream,
In this silent paradise.

Our breath hangs in the air,
Like whispers we can't hold,
Each moment we share,
A tale quietly told.

Through the cold we glide,
Two souls intertwined,
In this frozen tide,
A refuge we find.

Huddled Thoughts in the Silence

In the hush of the night,
Thoughts gather like frost,
Huddled close for warmth,
In silence, we are lost.

The moon casts silver beams,
Upon the sleeping trees,
While we talk of dreams,
And the soft winter breeze.

Every word a caress,
In the velvet dark,
With every shared stress,
We ignite a spark.

In the cradle of night,
Our secrets take flight,
Wrapped in soft stillness,
Our hearts feel just right.

Wreathe of Thawing Tendrils

As the sun starts to rise,
Winter begins to fade,
A wreathe of thawing sighs,
Nature's soft cascade.

Green shoots pierce the ground,
A promise of rebirth,
In the silence resound,
The echo of the earth.

Tender leaves unfurl,
In the warm embrace,
Of a brand new world,
In this sacred space.

With each gentle breath,
Life awakens anew,
In the dance of death,
Beauty shines through.

Embraced by Flame

In the ember's glow, we stand so near,
Whispers of warmth drown out the fear.
Flickering shadows dance on the wall,
Together we rise, together we fall.

Hearts intertwined, like smoke in the night,
Every heartbeat ignites, a passion, a light.
In the crackling fire, our dreams take flight,
Embraced by the flame, we burn ever bright.

Heartbeats Against the Chill

Cold winds howl through the barren trees,
Yet your heartbeat keeps me at ease.
Wrapped in silence, not a sound to break,
With each pulse, a promise, a bond we make.

Frost kisses the ground, a crisp twilight,
But in your arms, everything feels right.
Against the chill, our warmth ignites,
Heartbeats together, fueling the nights.

Sheltered from the Storm

Raindrops pitter-patter on the roof,
Inside our haven, we find our proof.
With every thunder, a heartbeat loud,
In this shared space, we're safely bowed.

Windows rattled by the tempest's call,
Yet love persists through it all.
In the chaos, our laughter rings,
Sheltered from storms, we find our wings.

Glacial Layers of Love

Beneath the surface, secrets lie deep,
Like glaciers waiting while the world sleeps.
Each layer tells a story, old yet new,
In the silence of ice, my heart calls for you.

We navigate slowly, with careful grace,
Unearthing treasures in this frozen space.
Through the cold, a warmth begins to unfurl,
Glacial layers of love, our precious pearl.

Flickering Flames of Heart

In shadows deep, embers glow,
Whispers of love, soft and slow.
Hearts ignite with each tender spark,
Lighting the way through the dark.

Beneath the stars, the warmth unfolds,
A flame of dreams, stories told.
Passion dances, fierce and bright,
Guiding us through the endless night.

With every breath, the fire grows,
In secret places, where love flows.
A flicker here, a blaze there,
In the stillness, we find our air.

Together we stand, hand in hand,
Creating a warmth, forever planned.
Flickering flames, a sacred art,
A beacon of love, the flickering heart.

Glacial Gardens of Warmth

In gardens where the cold winds blow,
Soft blooms rise through the frosty snow.
Petals open, kissed by the light,
Creating warmth in the chilling night.

Each breath a whisper, gently shared,
Amongst the blooms, hearts have bared.
Ice may surround, but love's embrace,
Transforms the cold into a warm space.

Winding paths of glacial grace,
Lead us through this tranquil place.
With every step, a love that stays,
In glacial gardens, warmth displays.

The chill retreats, as colors blend,
In beauty's hold, our hearts we send.
Through icy realms, our spirits twine,
In glacial gardens, love will shine.

Cocooning Comforts

Wrapped in warmth, we find our peace,
A tender space where worries cease.
In gentle folds, we're held so tight,
Cocooned in love, all feels so right.

The world outside may rush and roar,
But here, my dear, we need not score.
Soft whispers floated, dreams entwined,
In this embrace, true solace find.

Through softest threads, our hearts align,
Creating magic, yours and mine.
In quiet moments, we deeply dive,
Cocooning comforts, helping thrive.

With every sigh, our spirits soar,
In love's cocoon, we yearn for more.
Safety found in each other's gaze,
In cozy nooks, our hearts will blaze.

Hibernation of the Heart

In winter's grasp, the heart takes pause,
A time to dream, without a cause.
Under the snow, our feelings rest,
Awaiting spring, when we're our best.

Silent nights wrap us in peace,
Love's gentle warmth grants sweet release.
In stillness, hope begins to rise,
Awakening life beneath the skies.

Through icy breath, the heart will wait,
For sunlit days to unlock the gate.
Emerging stronger, from sleep we part,
Reviving whispers, a brand new start.

Hibernation yields to vibrant cheer,
As blossoms bloom, our truths grow clear.
With each new dawn, we find our way,
In the hibernation of the heart, we stay.

Solace in Hibernation

In the quiet of the night,
Dreams cocooned in soft white,
Nature slows, breath held tight,
Finding peace in winter's sight.

Beneath layers, life awaits,
Hope concealed, as stillness baits,
The heart finds rest, it curates,
Warmth within as cold abates.

Time unmoves, as shadows blend,
Silent whispers, nature's friend,
In the dark, we comprehend,
That all lives wait for spring's mend.

When the thaw begins to pour,
Life will burst, and spirits soar,
But for now, we just explore,
The solace here, forevermore.

Melting Permafrost

Whispers rise from frozen earth,
As seasons shift and find their birth,
Crystals melt, revealing worth,
In the thaw, we find rebirth.

Songs of rivers start to flow,
Beneath the sun's warm, golden glow,
Life awakens, starts to grow,
In the dance of ebb and flow.

Echoes of the past remain,
Frosted dreams, now love's refrain,
While the new begins to gain,
Nature's cycle, sweet and plain.

With every drop, the world renews,
Casting old layers, shedding blues,
In the light, where life imbues,
We find joy in every muse.

Warmth Beneath Starlit Skies

Underneath the cosmic dome,
Hearts entwined in twilight's warmth,
Whispers echo, love's sweet poem,
Beneath the stars, we find our home.

Night unfolds, a velvet shroud,
In the silence, dreams are loud,
With each breath, we feel endowed,
In this space where we're allowed.

Galaxies twinkle, stories told,
In the coolness, we are bold,
Finding comfort in the cold,
Canvas bright, our love unfolds.

Wishes cast with shooting stars,
Binding hearts like shining bars,
Underneath these ancient cars,
We find peace, just being ours.

Sheltered from the Silent Storm

Within the walls, the world concealed,
Raindrops dance, yet hearts are healed,
In this refuge, dreams are sealed,
While nature's rage is unconcealed.

The thunder rolls, a distant song,
Yet here we feel we both belong,
In the quiet, right and wrong,
Together, resilient and strong.

Windows frame the wild embrace,
As shadows move with gentle grace,
In the stillness, we find our place,
Safe from storms, we match the pace.

As winds howl, we share a glance,
In our shelter, love does dance,
Here we craft our tender chance,
In the storm, we find romance.

Whispered Fireside Dreams

In the glow of embers bright,
Soft whispers dance in the night,
Tales of joy and shadows tall,
Filling hearts, enchanting all.

Laughter mingles with the flame,
Memories linger, call by name,
A world outside fades away,
In this warmth, forever stay.

Cloaked in silence, soft and deep,
Secrets shared, promises keep,
Dreams unfurl like smoke anew,
In this circle, just me and you.

As the night gently unfolds,
Stories near, the fire holds,
With whispered dreams, we ignite,
A spark of love, our hearts alight.

Flickering Warmth in a Wintry Realm

Snowflakes drift on chilly air,
In the stillness, beauty rare,
A crackling fire, bright and bold,
Keeps us wrapped in joys untold.

Outside, a world dressed in white,
Inside, we share this cozy light,
With every flicker, warmth we find,
A sanctuary for the mind.

Windows frosted, hearts aglow,
Through the storm, we choose to grow,
Gathered close, our spirits soar,
In this realm, we yearn for more.

Time stands still, the night feels new,
In whispered dreams, we'll see it through,
A flickering warmth, our guiding star,
In a wintry realm, we've come so far.

Beneath the Glare and Sparkle

Stars above, a twinkling show,
Beneath the glare, soft winds blow,
Moments captured, hearts unfold,
Stories whispered, adventures told.

In the quiet, dreams ignite,
Underneath the moon's pure light,
Gentle laughter fills the air,
Joyful spirits everywhere.

Each spark a wish, a hope that gleams,
At midnight's hour, we chase our dreams,
With every glance, a tale begins,
In this dance, our journey spins.

Holding close each fleeting hour,
Within the glow, we find our power,
Beneath the glare, together we thrive,
In the sparkle of night, we come alive.

Comfort in the Chill

Cold winds howl, the night is long,
Yet here we're safe, where we belong,
Blankets wrapped, the fire warm,
In our hearts, we brave the storm.

Outside, frost bites at our feet,
Inside, the rhythm of hearts' beat,
Hot cocoa sipped in cozy cheer,
Moments treasured, loved ones near.

With every sigh, the world grows calm,
Each whispered word, a soothing balm,
In the chill, our dreams take flight,
Comfort reigns within this light.

Together we stand, hand in hand,
Facing the cold, we understand,
In every chill, a chance to feel,
In the warmth of love, our hearts reveal.

The Hearth's Gentle Lullaby

Flames dance in the twilight glow,
Whispers of warmth in the evening's flow.
Crisp air outside, but here we stay,
Wrapped in peace at the end of the day.

Sparks rise like dreams to the starry night,
Crackling sounds that feel just right.
Soft shadows flicker on the wall,
Embraced by love, we softly fall.

The world outside is cold and vast,
Yet here in comfort, troubles are cast.
Every heartbeat is a song,
In this lullaby, we belong.

As embers fade, night's whispers call,
In the hearth's glow, we cherish it all.
Together we drift, hearts intertwined,
In this gentle lullaby, serenity we find.

Winter's Secret Sanctuary

Snowflakes dance through the silent trees,
Nature whispers carried on the breeze.
In the stillness, a world remade,
Secrets hidden beneath the shade.

Icicles hang like crystal charms,
Embracing peace with winter's arms.
Footsteps crunch on a frosty path,
In this sanctuary, find the earth's calm bath.

The stars above in velvet skies,
Hiding wonders, a sweet surprise.
Here in winter's tender keep,
A place of magic, serene and deep.

Each breath a mist, a fleeting sigh,
In this sanctuary, dreams can fly.
Hold the moment, let it stay,
Winter's embrace, come what may.

Kindling Dreams in Frozen Times

Amidst the chill, where stillness reigns,
We gather warmth, igniting flames.
In frozen moments, dreams take flight,
Whispers of hope in the soft twilight.

The world outside, a canvas white,
Yet in our hearts, a spark of light.
Gathered close, we share our fears,
Through the darkness, we shed our tears.

With every flicker, stories weave,
In this cocoon, we dare believe.
Kindling visions of what could be,
In frozen times, we find our glee.

So let the winter winds blow strong,
In warmth and laughter, we belong.
Together we rise, together we shine,
Kindling dreams, forever entwined.

Soft Thaw of Tender Moments

As winter melts, the world unfolds,
Softthaw whispers, the heart beholds.
Petals budding, colors anew,
In tender moments, life breaks through.

Every drop of melting snow,
Brings forth laughter, bright and slow.
Nature's breath is sweet and warm,
In this shift, we feel the charm.

Sunlight spills on the waking ground,
In gentle silence, love is found.
Moments linger, soft and pure,
With every heartbeat, we're reassured.

Let us cherish this time of grace,
In the soft thaw, we find our place.
Together we write our own sweet song,
In tender moments, where we belong.

The Warmth of Togetherness

In the glow of laughter, we unite,
Hearts entwined, our spirits take flight.
With every shared story and gentle glance,
Together we weave a joyous dance.

The warmth of your presence, a comforting balm,
In this cozy haven, our love feels calm.
Through storms outside, we remain inside,
Wrapped in togetherness, no need to hide.

Every moment shared, a treasure we keep,
In the silence of night, our promises seep.
As candles flicker, shadows play,
In the warmth of togetherness, we find our way.

Wrapped in Winter Light

Snowflakes whisper secrets, soft and bright,
In this enchanting world, we take flight.
Wrapped in winter's embrace, we find our grace,
As magic unfolds in this frosty place.

The sun's gentle rays, a golden delight,
Dance on the snow, igniting the night.
With each step we take, the earth sparkles white,
Together we glow, wrapped in winter light.

Hot cocoa in hand, we savor the bliss,
With laughter that echoes, who could resist?
As frost paints the windows, a beautiful sight,
We hold each other close, wrapped in winter light.

Candlelit Comforts

In the flicker of candles, shadows sway,
Whispers of warmth, guiding our way.
A soft glow surrounds us, inviting and near,
Candlelit comforts, a moment to cheer.

With each gentle flame, our worries dissolve,
Creating a space where hearts can resolve.
As time slips away, we cherish the night,
In the warmth of the moment, everything feels right.

Stories are shared, wrapped in the glow,
Candlelit comforts, the love we bestow.
With every soft ember, our souls intertwine,
In this tranquil haven, forever you'll shine.

Chilling Beauty

In the stillness of night, the world breathes slow,
Chilling beauty surrounds, where cold winds blow.
The moon's silver light dances on the ground,
In every sharp breath, a new peace is found.

Frost-kissed branches in the pale moonlight,
Nature's artistry glimmers, a wondrous sight.
With every soft whisper of the winter breeze,
We find solace wrapped in the chill of the trees.

As we wander through this crystalline land,
Holding your warmth with a gentle hand.
Chilling beauty may bite, but love softly gleams,
In the heart of the cold, we fulfill our dreams.

Serene Warmth

In the gentle light of dawn,
The world begins to wake anew,
Soft whispers in the breeze,
Nature's touch, a tender clue.

Golden rays on dewy grass,
Morning's kiss, a sweet embrace,
Every leaf begins to dance,
In this quiet, perfect space.

Gentle hearts begin to grow,
With every moment, time slows down,
A calming peace, a soft glow,
In the warmth, we wear no frown.

Together, we find our place,
Where love and kindness intertwine,
In the serene, we trace our grace,
Forever yours, forever mine.

Winter's Warmest Secrets

Snowflakes fall in silent grace,
Covering the world in white,
Whispers of a soft embrace,
As day gives way to night.

In the hearth, the fire glows,
Casting shadows, tales unfold,
Winter's warmth in quiet shows,
Secrets in the stories told.

Frosted windows, a cozy sight,
Time to linger, wrap up tight,
Hot cocoa warms both heart and hand,
In this season, love will stand.

Let the chill outside remain,
Inside, hearts are free of strain,
In winter's grasp, we find our heat,
In softest moments, love's complete.

Firelit Reveries

Dancing flames paint the night,
Stories flicker in the dark,
Every crackle brings to light,
Memories that leave a mark.

Laughter echoes in the room,
Warmth spreads wider, hearts unite,
In the shadows, banish gloom,
Firelit dreams take glorious flight.

Let the world outside grow cold,
Here within, we are alive,
In this space, a bond unfolds,
In fire's glow, our spirits thrive.

As the embers softly fade,
Hold me close on this long night,
In the warmth, two hearts paraded,
Together strong, our love ignites.

Hushed Moments in December

December's breath is crisp and clear,
Whispers float on frosty air,
Every glance, a memory near,
In the stillness, moments spare.

Candles flicker in the gloom,
A soft glow that warms the soul,
In the heart, there lies a room,
Filled with love that makes us whole.

Hushed conversations by the fire,
Stories shared, hopes intertwine,
In this season, dreams aspire,
With you, all our hearts align.

When the snow begins to fall,
Nature's quilt, a pure embrace,
In these moments, we stand tall,
Hushed and cherished, love's sweet grace.

Tender Threads of Heat

In the quiet of the night,
A fire flickers bright,
Casting shadows on the wall,
Listening to the soft night call.

Warmth wraps around like a hug,
Drawing close, there's no shrug,
The world outside may chill and bite,
But here, hearts glow with light.

Memories dance in the air,
Laughter weaves everywhere,
With each smolder, love takes form,
In tender threads, we find warmth.

Embers fade, yet still we cling,
To the joys that flame can bring,
As long as we hold this dear,
The chill will never come near.

Winter's Embrace of Comfort

Snowflakes drift, soft and light,
Covering the ground in white,
Whispers of the cold wind call,
Yet inside, we feel no fall.

Hot cocoa warms each hand,
As cozy dreams begin to stand,
A blanket thick, wrapped up tight,
Nestled safe through the long night.

By the fire, stories flow,
Of seasons past, of joy and woe,
Together we watch the snowflakes swirl,
In winter's embrace, our hearts unfurl.

Time slows down, as we rest,
In moments shared, we are blessed,
For in this season's chilly grace,
We find our home in love's embrace.

The Light Beyond the Chill

Frosty breath hangs in the air,
Yet hope lingers everywhere,
For in the dark, a spark will shine,
A beacon bright, a promise divine.

Through the trees, a glow appears,
Chasing away our winter fears,
In every shadow, light shall play,
Guiding our hearts in a gentle way.

Stars above, like diamonds bright,
Lead us through the quiet night,
For every chill that comes our way,
There's warmth in love that's here to stay.

Hand in hand, we walk the trail,
With every step, we will prevail,
The light within shall always stay,
Filling our souls, come what may.

Glowing Hearts in the Winter Night

Underneath a velvet sky,
Glowing lights flicker and fly,
Every heartbeat sings a tune,
A lullaby beneath the moon.

In the hush, still moments breathe,
Wrapped in warmth, we take our leave,
From dappled paths and frosty air,
To embrace love, beyond compare.

With whispered dreams and softest sighs,
We share the stars that light our eyes,
Each glimmer a story, softly spun,
In this winter night, we are one.

As snowflakes fall, we remain near,
With glowing hearts, we cast out fear,
In this season, our souls ignite,
Together we shine, a brilliant light.

Gentle Heat

In the morning glow, a tender spark,
A warmth that lingers, soothing the dark.
Soft breezes carry, a fragrant tease,
Embraced in comfort, the heart finds ease.

Golden rays dance, upon the skin,
Whispers of summer, where dreams begin.
Nature's canvas, painted in light,
Gentle heat wraps the soul so tight.

Evening falls, a serenade sweet,
Stars awaken, to the rhythm of beat.
Under the sky, our stories unfold,
In gentle heat, our love grows bold.

Each moment cherished, no time to waste,
In this warm embrace, we find our place.
Together we wander, through life's warm stream,
Wrapped in gentle heat, living the dream.

Icy Bliss

Upon the glacier, where silence reigns,
Crystal shards gleam like intricate chains.
A world of wonder, untouched and free,
Icy bliss calls, as wild as the sea.

Frosted whispers weave through the air,
Snowflakes descend, like a tender prayer.
In stillness, beauty, a captivating sight,
Icy bliss holds the heart tight tonight.

Under the moon, the landscape glows,
In winter's arms, where adventure flows.
Each breath of chill, awakens the soul,
In icy bliss, we become whole.

Skates carve the ice, in flowing design,
Dancing with shadows, we intertwine.
Together we laugh, as snowflakes fall,
In icy bliss, we conquer it all.

Whispered Joy

In quiet moments, love softly speaks,
With every glance, the heart gently peaks.
Whispers of joy, like a breeze in spring,
Filling the air, with what happiness brings.

Laughter dances, upon the sweet air,
A melody found, beyond compare.
In shared secrets, a bond so tight,
Whispered joy glows, in the soft twilight.

Memories linger, warm like the sun,
In this embrace, we are forever one.
Through life's chapters, hand in hand,
Whispered joy guides, as we both stand.

With gentle voices, our dreams take flight,
In whispered joy, the world feels right.
Together we journey, hearts open wide,
In this whispered joy, love is our guide.

Serendipity in Solitude

In quiet stillness, treasures await,
Moments of peace, where we contemplate.
Serendipity blooms, in twilight's embrace,
Finding ourselves, in our own sacred space.

Among the shadows, soft thoughts arise,
A dance with dreams under starlit skies.
In solitude's arms, we learn to be free,
Serendipity calls, just you and me.

Nature's whispers, a tender caress,
In solitude found, we find our best.
Each heartbeat echoes, a beautiful song,
In this quiet realm, we both belong.

So here's to the moments, we quietly seek,
In serendipity, our souls softly speak.
Together we wander, through pathways of thought,
In solitude's grace, true happiness is wrought.

Glowing Coals and Snowy Whispers

The fire flickers, softly bright,
Glowing coals in the fading night.
Outside, the world wears a blanket white,
Whispers of snow in quiet flight.

Embers dance in a warm embrace,
Nature sleeps in a frozen grace.
Together they share the night's soft pace,
Coals and snowflakes, a gentle chase.

Branches bow with their icy load,
While the hearth sings a soothing ode.
In this moment, warmth bestowed,
Hearts find comfort on the road.

Silent thoughts as shadows creep,
Glowing coals cradle secrets deep.
In this calm, our dreams we keep,
Winter's breath, a lullaby's sweep.

Together in the Frost's Caress

In the chill where the whispers play,
Frost paints silver on branches sway.
Hand in hand as we find our way,
Together, in night's soft array.

The moonlight casts a gentle glow,
Footprints echo in the soft, white snow.
Winter's breath is a sweetened flow,
Hearts entwined in the night's throe.

Stars twinkle like diamonds afar,
Guiding us beneath the night's star.
As we stroll, it feels like a memoir,
Frozen moments, love's memoir.

Wrapped in layers, so warm, so near,
Together, we conquer every fear.
In the frost, we find cheer,
An embrace that draws us here.

Frosted Embrace

Soft daylight dims where shadows linger,
Whispers of frost thread through our fingers.
Each breath forms clouds as hope sings clearer,
Frosted embrace, the heart's true mirror.

Beneath the trees where silence reigns,
Snowflakes dance on the gentle plains.
Together we share all joys and pains,
In every heartbeat, love's refrain.

Icicles hang like crystal tears,
But together we've conquered our fears.
In the stillness, the warmth appears,
A bond so strong, it heavenly steers.

In the frosted air, we find our place,
Locked in love's tender embrace.
Through every season, every trace,
Together we rise, a timeless grace.

Hearthside Whispers

By the fire, where spirits lift,
Hearthside whispers, a precious gift.
The shadows flicker as hearts drift,
In cozy warmth, our thoughts will sift.

Softly crackles the burning flame,
Each ember a tale, no two the same.
In the glow, we play love's sweet game,
A tapestry stitched with laughter's name.

Outside the winds howl, fierce and wild,
But here, serenity's gentle child.
In the warmth, our souls compiled,
Amidst the hissing, cold and riled.

As stars peer down, in silent awe,
Hearthside whispers breathe a soft law.
In every moment, in every flaw,
We weave a world without a draw.

Cozy Ember Glow

In the hearth, the embers sigh,
Crackling softly, time slips by.
Shadows dance upon the wall,
Whispers linger, as night falls.

A warm embrace, a gentle start,
Each flicker warms the weary heart.
Together, we watch the fire's thread,
In this glow, our worries shed.

The scent of cedar fills the air,
Moments treasured, beyond compare.
In this nook, we find our place,
Cozy embers, a warm embrace.

As time drifts on, we won't forget,
The warmth we shared, the dreams we met.
In this space, the world feels right,
Cozy ember glow, our hearts alight.

A Blanket of Silence

Underneath the silver sky,
A blanket of silence drifts nigh.
Whispers of snow upon the ground,
In this stillness, peace is found.

Footsteps muffled, soft and light,
Nature's canvas, pure and white.
Every flake a tale to tell,
In this hush, we know it well.

The world fades under frosted breath,
Quiet echoes that dance with death.
Yet in this void, we can embrace,
A blanket of silence, a sacred space.

Together we walk, side by side,
Finding solace, love as our guide.
In the quiet, hearts align,
A blanket of silence, forever divine.

Frost-Kissed Solace

Beneath the trees, the frost lies deep,
In icy charms, the world does sleep.
A crystal blanket, cold and pure,
Frost-kissed solace, hearts endure.

Branches glisten with diamond grace,
Nature's beauty, a sacred space.
In the stillness, moments freeze,
Frost-kissed solace, quiet ease.

Footprints mark our gentle path,
Warmth ignites in winter's wrath.
Together we forge memories bright,
In this solace, hearts take flight.

As evening falls, a perfect hue,
Stars awaken, shining through.
In frost's embrace, we find our way,
Frost-kissed solace, night and day.

Heartfire in the Haze

In the twilight, warmth ignites,
Heartfire glows, banishing frights.
Embers flicker in the mist,
Moments cherished, not to be missed.

Through the haze, we weave our dreams,
In the quiet, love redeems.
A flickering dance, we hold on tight,
Heartfire burning, pure delight.

In this haze, the world feels light,
Filling darkness with brilliant sight.
Together we stand, hearts ablaze,
In the warmth of the heartfire's haze.

As night embraces the fading day,
In heartfire's glow, we find our way.
A bond eternal, forever grows,
Heartfire in the haze, love flows.

Firelight and Feathers

Dancing flames in the hush of night,
Whispers of warmth in the flickering light.
Feathers drift softly, carried by dreams,
A world born anew in the fire's gleams.

Echoes of stories, old and profound,
In the hearth's embrace, a love is found.
Embers crackle, tales come alive,
Under the stars, our spirits thrive.

Shadows twist in a delicate play,
While time melts slowly, night turns to day.
Firelight flickers, memories soar,
Feathers and warmth, forevermore.

In the quiet, hearts gently sway,
Wrapped in the glow, we find our way.
Together we dance, in starlit embrace,
Lost in the magic, a sacred space.

The Blanket of Solace

A blanket of silence, wrapped tight around,
Comfort and stillness, in whispers profound.
Stars twinkle softly, in velvety skies,
Cradled in darkness, our worries subside.

Trees sway gently, a lullaby played,
The world feels at peace, in twilight's cascade.
Moonlight like silver, caresses the ground,
In night's gentle arms, our hearts are unbound.

Every soft rustle, each sigh in the air,
The blanket of solace, a tender affair.
Moments like treasures, forever we'll keep,
Cradled in comfort, we drift into sleep.

Lost in the magic, in shadows we dwell,
Wrapped in the night, we cast our own spell.
With dreams as our guide, we'll wander and roam,
In the blanket of solace, we always feel home.

Frost Kisses

Whispers of winter, a kiss on the cheek,
Frost paints the world, so quiet, so meek.
Stars shine like diamonds, the moon's gentle gaze,
In the chill of the night, our hearts set ablaze.

Footprints in snow, a story unfolds,
Nature's fond secrets, in silence retold.
Trees wear their crystals, a delicate dress,
Wrapped in white whispers, the earth's sweet caress.

Warmth from within, in the frosty embrace,
Our laughter like music, a timeless grace.
With each frosty kiss, there's magic to find,
In the chill of the night, our spirits aligned.

Each flake is a promise, a gift from above,
In the quiet of winter, we find peace and love.
Frost kisses linger, a memory made,
In the heart of the night, we're never afraid.

Heart Glows

In the soft light of dawn, our hopes take flight,
Hearts intertwined as we greet the sunlight.
Every moment cherished, like petals in bloom,
Love's gentle touch dispels all the gloom.

Laughter like echoes, bright as the day,
In the warmth of connection, worries decay.
We gather our dreams, like fireflies bright,
Together we dance in the glow of the light.

With each passing hour, our spirits align,
A tapestry woven, so richly designed.
Through storms and through shadows, we rise with grace,

In the light of our hearts, we all find our place.

As the sun dips low, and twilight descends,
The glow of our hearts will never see ends.
With whispered affirmations, we've chosen this way,
In harmony's warmth, forever we'll stay.

Cotton Clouds and Ember Nights

Cotton clouds drift in a canvas of blue,
Painting the sky with softest of hues.
Embers are glowing, a promise of light,
While whispers of dreams dance with the night.

Waves of warm colors, the sunset bestows,
In the twilight's embrace, our laughter flows.
Time slows its march as we savor the scene,
In cottony softness, our hearts are serene.

Stars twinkle bright as night gently falls,
In the embered glow, we hear nature's calls.
Together we wander, both lost and found,
In the magic of moments, forever unbound.

With each breath of night and each shimmer of light,
We weave our own stories, pure and so bright.
In the canvas above, our wishes take flight,
On cotton clouds softly, through embered night.

Thawing Moments

In the hush of dawn's embrace,
Nature stirs with gentle grace.
Whispers of spring in the air,
Icicles melt, shedding despair.

Golden rays begin to peek,
Life awakens, soft and meek.
Every bud a promise made,
In warmth, the chill will soon cascade.

Birds return with songs so sweet,
On the ground, the soft grass greets.
Moments passing, hearts ignite,
In the thaw, we find our light.

Hands entwined, we stroll and smile,
As winter fades, let's stay awhile.
Each breath filled with hope and cheer,
In our souls, the spring is near.

Warmth Beneath the Ice

Beneath the frosty crystal sheen,
Life hides softly, yet unseen.
Under layers, stories flow,
Memories from long ago.

The river's pulse, a steady beat,
In its depths, the warmth we seek.
Underneath the hardened crust,
Lies the promise, pure and just.

With each crack, the echoes sing,
Hope returns with the coming spring.
Softly thawing, dreams take flight,
Under ice, our hearts feel light.

In the silence, secrets breathe,
Renewal waits, a gentle wreathe.
As layers fade, life reappears,
In the warmth, we shed our fears.

Glimmers of Comfort

Stars above in velvet skies,
Glimmers of hope catch our eyes.
In the night, the world feels wide,
Comfort finds us, warmth inside.

Whispered dreams like fireflies,
Dancing 'neath the moonlit sighs.
Every glow a gentle spark,
Leading us through the deep dark.

Hands that meet under the light,
Bringing solace from the night.
Hearts entwined, a sacred space,
In the stillness, we find grace.

In the shadows, hope ascends,
Through the gloom, our spirit bends.
Glimmers shine like distant shores,
Guiding us to open doors.

Icy Moonlight

Moonlight dances on the frost,
Illuminating paths we've crossed.
Silver beams on frozen streams,
Whisper secrets, weave our dreams.

In the stillness of the night,
Icy patterns catch the light.
With each step, the world feels bright,
Wrapped in winter's pure delight.

Stars like diamonds in the sky,
Reflect our wishes, soaring high.
Underneath this chilling glow,
Hearts beat warm, love's ember glows.

As the night begins to wane,
We embrace the soft refrain.
Moonlight fades, yet still we see,
In this magic, you and me.

Fiery Hearts

Two souls join in blazing dance,
Igniting flames with every glance.
Passion's warmth, a gentle spark,
  Kindles light within the dark.

In the night, we fan the embers,
In our hearts, the fire remembers.
With every laugh, with every sigh,
  The heat between us can't deny.

Days turn cold, yet here we stand,
  Fierce and brave, hand in hand.
Through the storms, our spirits fly,
Like burning coals against the sky.

Love's inferno, fierce and free,
  In its glow, we simply be.
Fiery hearts will never tire,
  Together, we ignite the fire.

Milton Keynes UK
Ingram Content Group UK Ltd.
UKHW021240191124
451300UK00007B/160

9 789916 944325